Enjoy the tea party -

Deann Heckim

Dedicated to children everywhere

Text and illustrations for Tea With the Angels ©2008

by Leann Hechim
illustrations by Arthur Price

ISBN 978-0-692-00054-0

Published by Seven Angels Publishing

Printed in the United States of America

Please visit the author's web site:
www.teawiththeangels.com

Tea With the Angels

by Leann Hechim
illustrations by Arthur Price

Summer was filled with sunshine and free time, but best of all for Carolyn and Catherine summer was filled with weekends with Grandma and Grandpa in the country.

Grandma and Grandpa's house was warm and inviting, but almost better than that was the sisters' own playhouse that stood at the end of a winding path. Carolyn and Catherine spent endless hours running back and forth from one house to the other.

Every night just before bedtime, Grandma and Grandpa would gather the girls to read them a story about angels. But these were not just ordinary angels. They were the very special Angels of Mother Nature.

When Catherine and Carolyn fell asleep, the

Angels often visited them in their dreams.

One special morning as she woke up Catherine said to Carolyn, "Last night I had a dream about a tea party with the Angels right in our playhouse."

"Me too!" Carolyn exclaimed. "All of the angels were there!"

Dressing quickly, the girls ran to the kitchen for breakfast.

"The Angels are coming to our playhouse for a tea party this morning!" Catherine said, excitedly.

"How wonderful! Tea with the Angels!" said Grandma.

Carolyn and Catherine gathered up their most special tea set, a gift from Grandma and Grandpa, and headed off down the winding path to set up their tea party.

First to arrive was the Earthly Mother. When the girls opened the door, a pure, white, shimmering light filled the doorway. The Mother Angel was radiant and beautiful, just as they had seen her in their dreams.

Mother Nature extended her hands to the girls and spoke softly, "Hello, dear ones."

"Oh, please come in, Earthly Mother," they said delightedly. 'We've been waiting for you."

After serving the Angel tea, Carolyn poured a cup for herself and her sister. The Earthly Mother took a sip and set her cup down on the table.

"I am so happy to be here today," she said. "But do you know that my Angels and I are really always with you, every day and every night? Even if you can't see us with your eyes, we are still here."

"Grandma reminds us of that every night!" shared Carolyn.

"Today we have come to teach you about the gifts we bring each and every day," the Earthly Mother explained.

"But where are the other Angels?" the two sisters asked together.

The white shimmering Angel pointed to the window where the early morning sun was peeking through the curtains.

"Look girls. The Angel of Sun is here."

The girls marveled at the light as it filtered through the trees and danced on top of the stream.

Catherine and Carolyn turned and rushed out the door with the Earthly Mother right behind them.

"Hello sweet ones," said the Angel of Sun as she made her way to the edge of the bridge. "I shed my golden light every day – rain or shine. The gift I have for you is light and warmth. My light allows you to see everything on this beautiful Earth."

"Oh! Then you mean, you are shining everyday no matter what!" Catherine realized.

"That's right," replied the Angel.

"Thank you, Angel of Sun," said Carolyn. "Would you like to come to our tea party?"

"I wouldn't miss it for the world," smiled the Angel.

Just as they reached the bridge, the Earthly Mother stopped and pointed, "Look, girls."

"Angel of Water! We're having a tea party, and we'd like you to come and join us," said Carolyn.

"I'd be delighted to join you, but first let me tell you why I'm here," said the Angel of Water. "I provide the drinking water you need every day to keep your bodies healthy and growing. I'm also here as rain for watering the Earth so everything can grow."

On their way back to the playhouse, the Earthly Mother stopped again and pointed at the wind chimes ringing in the tree, and said, "Girls, I'd like you to meet the next Angel."

"Hello, Carolyn and Catherine, I'm the Angel of Air," greeted the new Angel.

"Hello, Angel of Air. We almost didn't see you" said the girls. "You are nearly invisible!"

"Come and share your swing. I want to show you something," said the lovely Angel.

The girls sat side by side while the Earthly Mother pushed them higher and higher.

"Do you feel me as you swing back and forth?" the Angel of Air asked.

"Oh, yes," they said.

"You feel like a soft brush on my face and through my hair." described Catherine.

"I'm here so that you can breathe. Your bodies must have air in order to stay alive and be healthy. Now take a deep breath in and hold it for a second, then let it out slowly," she said. "And now would you do that again?"

"I feel so calm," said Carolyn smiling.

"Won't you join us for tea?" asked Catherine heading toward the playhouse.

But before the Angel of Air could answer, the girls noticed another Angel crouched in the vegetable garden.

"Good morning dear ones," she said waving to the girls. "I am the Angel of Earth. I am the beloved ground you walk on, always under you for support."

The girls reached down and brushed their hands on the dirt path at their feet.

"Would you like to come inside for our tea party now?" invited Carolyn.

The Angel of Earth and the girls stood and walked out of the garden.

Catherine and Carolyn were very excited. There were now five Angels coming to tea.

Just as Carolyn opened the door to the playhouse, the Mother Angel said, "Wait girls, there are two more Angels. I would like you to meet the Angel of Life and the Angel of Joy. Let's find them before we begin our tea party."

"More Angels!" exclaimed the sisters. "This is so wonderful! But where are they?"

The Earthly Mother closed her eyes and held her arms out in front of her. A second later, the Angel of Life appeared among the clouds. She was dressed like a butterfly, with beautiful wings the color of a rainbow.

"Hello, Catherine and Carolyn. I am the Angel of Life." The sisters stared with wide eyes at the beautiful Angel as she touched the ground before them. "Do you know that life is very precious?" she asked.

"Yes," Catherine replied. "We are always careful with living things even bugs."

"That is wonderful," said the Angel of Life. "I am here to help you know that your life is very precious as well. It is important to learn to love yourself all the time. Even if you are sad or angry," the Angel of Life explained.

"But it is hard to feel love when I'm mad," Carolyn sighed.

"I know, but those are the times that it is most important to remember to love yourself," responded the Angel of Life taking Carolyn's hand.

"Please join us," invited Catherine taking the Angel of Life's other hand.

"I'd be so happy to come to your tea party, my dear girls," the Angel of Life said. "But remember there is one more Angel to meet."

"The Angel of Joy!" cried the girls with delight.

In a puff of pink clouds, the Angel of Joy appeared. "Hello girls! I help you in feeling joy every day," the Angel said. "You will feel joy when you are doing what you love to do."

"Like when I sing!" exclaimed Catherine.

"Yes," said the Angel of Joy. "You will also feel joy when you are helping others."

"Oh, this is so fun to have tea with the Angels!" both girls grinned.

Carolyn, Catherine and all seven Angels

After everyone was seated, the Earthly Mother

"The Angels are always with us. The
We must always try to

"Even when we don't see the Angels,
at anytime and in any

entered the playhouse for their tea party.

asked the girls if they understood the Angels.

Angels help us in everything we do in life.
remember that," said Carolyn.

they are still with us. We can call on them
place," followed Catherine.

"Wonderful! Please close your eyes," the Earthly Mother said as they all put their cups down. "We want you to always remember that even when you don't see us we are here."

The Angel of Sun spoke next, "I am always shining upon you and within you."

"I provide the water that you, the animals, and our great Earth need to live and grow," said the Angel of Water.

"I help you remember to breathe deeply and to stay calm," said the Angel of Air.

"I give solid support to you and all the creatures and plants of the Earth," said the Angel of Earth.

"I help you remember to always love yourself no matter what," said the Angel of Life.

"I am here to remind you that you have precious gifts to give to others and to the world," said the Angel of Joy.

And then the Mother Angel said, "Again last, but not least, we are always with you. We love and bless you."

When Catherine and Carolyn opened their eyes, the Angels had disappeared. The girls could still feel the Angels in the room, and smiled knowing that the Angels would always be there for them.